THE BOOK OF JAMES

X-RAY FINDING PURPOSE IN PAIN

By James Brant III

James Brant III

Rackhouse Publishing
Read to Learn, Write to Remember

Published by: Rackhouse Publishing
Cover designed by: Nathan Mitchell
Page composition & Interior designed by: Rackhouse Publishing

ISBN: 9 78-0-9995384-6-3

For information about custom editions, special sales, premium
and corporate purchases, please contact:
JB3 Ministries | 904.274.1711 | www.jb3ministries.com

First Edition
Printed in the U.S.A

The Book of James

DEDICATION

This book is dedicated to my father, James Brant Jr., undoubtedly the most incredible man on the planet and the most incredible man in my life. To many who knew him, knew him as bishop, apostle, or even "Boo, but to me, he was just "DADDY" and that trumps everything else. The greatest possession or inheritance my father could've ever given me besides his name was his God. Thanks daddy. Love you insurmountably!

CONTENTS

ACKNOWLEDGMENTS

"Where there is no counsel, the people fall; But in the multitude of counselors there is safety." Proverbs 11:14 NKJV

First, I really want to thank God, because we have been in this thing called "My Life" together since day one. He has been my everything; not only my creator, my Savior and redeemer, but my joy, my comforter, my sustainer, my friend, and also sometimes my aggravation and disappointment, and I am very sure that I have been all of that last part and more to Him on this journey as well.

I want to thank my darling wife of sixteen years, Alneshia. Thank you for believing in me and sticking by me in spite of me. You've seen something in me that I couldn't see in myself, and sometimes maybe not knowing how to convey it to me, you just stayed with me to see it manifest to me through me. I love you very very very much. To our very handsome son Quad; you are indeed a daily reminder of the awesomeness of God. You are an incredible soldier. I love you more than words could ever say.

I want to also take this time to thank my parents; my father, the late James Brant, Jr. and my beautiful mother, Denise M. Brant for so much more than I could ever write in this book; your prolific wisdom; your awesome and consistent example; the many, and I really do mean many days of chastisement (whoopings/killings); the opportunities you have given us and the legacy you have left for us. You have been the epitome of parents, and I will forever be thankful for that alone. I love you. To all of my brothers, Lamar, Jerry, Daniel, David, Steven, Jerome and Ray; I couldn't have asked for better brothers. We never had to have outside friends because we've always had each other. To my sisters-in-law, Jackie, Dishan, Ciara, Kia and Jessica, I could never forget y'all. I love y'all too. To my nieces; Azariah, Jayde, Leilonii, Nalanii, Brooke, and Erin, and to my nephews; T.J., Daniel, Jayden, Jerry Jr., William, and A.J., and Kayden; I love y'all.

To my parents-in-law; y'all are just the two most coolest in-laws I've ever had. You have been there and done more than you were obligated to do. Thank you and I love you. To my grandmother, Thelma Louise

Brant; none of us would even be here had it not been for you. I love you so much. To all my uncles, aunts, and my entire family…, truly blood is thicker than water. To my Godmother, Mattie Strong, you are indeed a jewel; priceless.

I want to especially thank my church family, the Zarephath Tabernacle Church; the place that I serve every week. You are the most amazing group of people. To our school, Zarephath Academy; staff and students, I love you guys. To Bishop Willie Mincey and family, Bishop Lewis Williams, Dr. Terrance Calloway, Bishop Gentle L. Groover, Sr., Dr. Timothy Groover, Bishop Billy White, Bishop Joseph and Lady Derree Braswell, Apostle Lillie Tuggerson, Bishop Joseph Edge, Apostle Donald and Lady Vanessa Dubois and the entire Zarephath Kingsland, GA family, Bishop Leonard Gibbs, Prophet Albert McLeod, Bishop Anthony Chavers, Dr. Gregory Nelson, Pastor Russell Williams, Pastor Marc Dickerson, Pastor Jared Williams, Lorne Ruise, Verto and Angela Drayton, Perrier Williams, NeNe Callender, Lucy and Alex Hill, Meka Rollins, Darian and Michella Daniel, my cousins,

Pastor William and Dot Bradley and the New Hope Baptist Church family in Deltona Florida, Dr. Rolous Frazier and the St. John Missionary Baptist Church family in Orlando, FL and so many other names I can't fit them all in here.

An old friend would always tell me, "Proper People Placement Prevents Problems." In other words, everyone in your life whether good or bad has value, but it is where you place them in your life that will determine how valuable they are and what value they add to your life. So I want to say thank you to everyone for the part that you have played in my life. This road has not been easy by far, but the truth is it could've been much worst if you weren't there to help steer me toward my destiny. Thank you.

THE BOOK OF JAMES

X-RAY

FINDING PURPOSE IN PAIN

FOREWORD
†Leonard L. Gibbs, Jr., TH.D., D.D.

Jennie B. Wilson penned as lyrics in her song, *"Time is filled with swift transition…"* No matter your walk of life, we can all relate to these melodic sentiments.

When my children were smaller, there was an annual event that I would take them to; the county fair. The lights, popcorn, cotton candy, fairest wheels, roller coasters, stuffed animals, and other attractions always intrigued our interest to attend every year. As toddlers, when I would take them to the county fair, they enjoyed the treats and the rides that catered to toddlers. It was fun for them and stress free for me. However, as they got older, the tea cups, carousel, and pony rides that were once adventurous for them now became boring. They wanted to ride the roller coaster, the wipe-out, the dizzy dinosaur, the flying pirate ship, and the air swings. One year while at the fair, my son Christian said to me, "Pop, I want to ride the wipe-out."For those of you who are unfamiliar with this ride, it is designed to give the appearance that you riding this electronic surfboard, and you encountering some pretty strong waves. Sounds like fun, huh? To watch it is intriguing until it catches your attention, and makes you want the ride to experience the wipe out well at least you think you do. It wasn't until my son and I got on the ride that we discovered why they called it the "wipe-out". The ride starts out extremely calm and it gives you the same feeling you might feel if you felt like trying your hand at surfing. We started to feel little sensations as if we were actually surfing some waves, it was cool. The Beach Boys' song "Surfing USA" was blasting in the background. I looked at Christian and he was smiling with amazement. Then, all of a sudden, it happened! A major wave hit our electronic surfboard, and the impact made us feels as we where going in air to have an intimate conversation with the constellations. In an instant everyone's sense of ease was immediately turn into panic. I can still hear the screams of utter terror. As the sensation of the waves on this electrical ride grew stronger, so did the emotions of everyone's fear. I looked at Christian, and he said to me "Daddy, tell them to stop it." I said to him, "But son, you were so sure you wanted this ride." Christian said, "Daddy, I don't want it. Please make them stop it." Then I said to him, "Son, you're here now. It's not that simple." He screamed, "Daddy, I can't do this." I assured him, "Son, yes you can, take my hand."Christian took my hand, and as if my hand had some agent within it to calm him down, he immediately relaxed, although for another two minutes or so, which probably seemed like a lifetime to him in the moment, he remained calm. The electrical waves kept giving that sensation of us being cast into the air violently, but this time instead of panicking, he would squeeze my hand. Eventually, the ride was over, and we got off with Christian's hand still in mine. His sisters then came over, and they became intrigued with the "wipe-out" and asked if they could ride. Christian said, "That ride is scary, but don't go on it unless you take daddy with you."

In this amazing book written by my friend James Brant, he transparently reveals to us through his personal journey, how he and his wife, Alneshia had to ride their own personal "wipe-out". He meticulously straps us into our seats, and with his masterful description of the events, emotions, and encounters of his personal experience, we get to feel every wave with he, Alneshia, and Quad. He surfs through the swift transitions of time that attempt to wipe them out. He holds our hands firmly, gently walking us through every bump, bruise, and break that we all experience; and even navigating us through his personal experiences.

This book offers healing to the hearts of those who have been the casualty of a father's irresponsibility, by showing us how a father loves, learns, and lives through their "wipe-out" experiences. And through this narrative, we are able to better assess and appreciate the commitment of a father, who takes that scary ride through life with their child, and stays with them until the ride is completed.

This book helps us to really discover the lessons that pain teaches, and uncover the heroes within that that hurt creates. It is a book of reassurance that no matter what we face within our lives; regardless as to how scary, unexpected, unfortunate, or unfair it seems, God grants you the grace to stand and survive. When the "wipe-out" is over; at the conclusion of this book, you will be able to tell your friends as well don't take this ride without your father.

James Brant III

INTRODUCTION

Wow! Where do I even start? First of all, let me say this: if someone would have told me twelve years ago that I would be sitting here right now in a little downtown restaurant writing a book, I wouldn't have believed it in a million years (nor could I have even imagined it for that matter). But now know that the things that God takes you through to be you are God-designed, and tailor-made with no need for any alterations later! It's all for the purpose of blessing someone else…Can someone say guinea pig?

I will never forget a sermon I preached at my church when I was maybe about twenty-one years old. I was very young in ministry at that time. I had only been preaching maybe a year or so. I cannot remember exactly the title of my sermon that night. I was preaching about suffering, and how we must go through our trials. As a young preacher just happy for the opportunity to preach at all, there wasn't much for me to say and so I was simply preaching what I had heard my father and other older preachers preach about. I tuned, I whooped, I even hollered, "High five your neighbor and tell them this; shake three people's hand and tell them that…" The people were praising God, shouting, and dancing all over the church. It was awesome-or so I thought.

Later that night after I was done preaching and the service had ended; after some of our members came over and congratulated me on a job well done, hugs, encouraging words, and pats on the back, my father then calls me into his office. I walked into his office and sat down in the chair across the desk from him. He leaned back in his chair behind his desk looking up at the ceiling with this little funny smirk on his face. The office was silent for a minute or two. And as I was sitting there, I'm thinking to myself that he was about to tell me how I did an awesome job, and how I allowed the Lord to really used me, and how proud he was of me, and maybe I would even get a little love offering as well. My father sat up in his chair still with that little funny smirk still on his face, and said to me, "Son…," holding back the little chuckle in his voice, "When in the world have you ever suffered? Boy, you still live in my house! You've never suffered a day in your life. Son, you have no idea what suffering is. You've never had to pay to keep the lights on. You've never spent a night in the dark unless the power went out over the whole neighborhood. You've never had to sleep a night outside. You don't have that kind of testimony yet." Oh my God, y'all. My pride was so hurt and I felt so small. I felt like an ant that got sat on by an elephant. "Son, you sounded real good, and you're gonna be a good preacher one day, but never preach where you've never been," he said. "What makes a good preacher is when he has been through what he's talking about. And when he has been through what he's talking about, he can effectively tell others how to come through what he has been through. My father had been preaching since he was nineteen years old and pastored his first church at twenty-two years old. "Son, David could never have written the 23rd Psalm had he not experienced it first," he explained. My father would seemingly always have the tendency to bust your bubble or take all the wind out of your sail, but truthfully, he was just giving you wisdom today for the inevitabilities of tomorrow. That's my dad!

That was then; this is now. I'm now thirty-nine years old; eighteen years later, and if I was given the same opportunity to preach that same exact sermon again right now, it would certainly be much different than before. By this time, I have lived a little more. I have experienced some things, but most of all, I really learned who God is through it all. If my father were here today, I am certain that that the funny little smirk on his face from back then would be a huge smile of pride by now.

My name is James Brant III. My beautiful wife, Alneshia; (everybody calls her Neshia) and I have been married now for sixteen years. We also have an adorable thirteen year old son who is indeed my namesake, James IV. He is affectionately known by everyone as "Quad". Some have concluded that Quad has a disability, but we have concluded that he simply has a different ability. He is truly one of my greatest inspirations for this book.

As you read the Book of James, I share my entire journey with you in each chapter; my challenges, my struggles, my tragedies as well as my triumphs. Somehow I managed to survive and found purpose in my pain, and it is my honest and sincere prayer that everyone who reads this book will do the same. Welcome to my journey.

"But we have this treasure in earthen vessels, that the excellency of the power may be of God and not of us. We are hard-pressed on every side, yet not crushed; we are perplexed, but not in despair; persecuted, but not forsaken; struck down, but not destroyed"

2 Corinthians 4:7-9 NKJV

Who Did Sin?

(The Blame Game)

Master, who did sin, this man, or his parents, that he was born blind?" John 9:2 KJV

John 9 is a very special scripture to my family and I, in so much that there is hardly a day that goes by that we're not reminded of it. I am a firm believer that the Word of God can be, or in fact will remain of none effect until the reader places him or herself in the book, on the page, in the chapter, in the verse, and in the passage of that that he or she reads. If we are not careful, the Bible, His story can become merely reduced to just history. This is why the Hebrew writer admonished us of that in Hebrews.

> *"we ought to give the more earnest heed to the things which we have heard lest at any time we should let them slip."*
>
> Hebrews 2:1 KJV

John 9 is an encouraging story to us, because it shines a bright light on a revelation. It gives us hope in knowing that everything that happens to all of us in life is not always our fault. The light it brings destroys the relevance of an old Jewish belief . It was believed among the Jews that a man's condition, illness, or deficiency was a result of his or her sin, or their parents' sin. For instance, remember the story of Bartimaeus in the Gospel of Mark 10? For those of you who have never heard this story, he was a blind beggar. Did you know that Bartimaeus was not even this man's name? Mark 10 only gave to us the knowledge of who he belonged to, and as a result, he was a direct product of a very dysfunctional situation. Timaeus was his father's name, and his father's name means polluted. The word "Bar" means the son of; Bar-Timaeus. In essence, this man; this son was not even given his own identity, but is forced by the authority of the writer (Mark), as an adult, to still be labeled by his father's name and dysfunctional situation. My point is this: it wasn't this man's fault!

Here is another one! David prayed to God in the 51st Psalm, *"Wash me thoroughly from mine iniquity…"* Why? Because *"…I was shapen in iniquity; and in sin did my mother conceive me."* The word iniquity means the result of, or punishment for. Another definition is to be bent or twisted toward. David understood that who he was, the way he was, and what he had done was a reflection of his origin or conception; it began when he was conceived in sin. He prayed for forgiveness and freedom from the way he was. He asked God for a clean heart and a renewed spirit. David attempted to put the blame on himself, but in actuality, it wasn't his fault. He didn't have a chance. Here is where our story begins…

Nothing makes a man happier than to have a son to carry on his name and legacy. Having a son in the Bible was always a sign that God favored your house. At one point my wife and I were trying to have a child for two years without any success. People would always tell us, "When you're trying to have a baby, it almost never happens when you

"When you're trying to have a baby, it almost never happens when you want it to; it's when you stop trying that it always seems to happen, unexpectedly…"

want it to; it's when you stop trying that it always seems to happen unexpectedly…" My father said to us one day, "This baby that you want will come through much prayer." Not knowing at the time what he meant by that, we continued on with our lives, ministry, and everything else. I guess they all were right!

In February 2006, when Neshia and I were four months expecting, the gynecologist told us that there were some problems seen on the sonogram. The doctor went on to mention that we needed to be aware of the concerns related to our unborn baby boy. After hearing the news we were referred to the Regional Obstetric Consultants for high risk pregnancy issues. Things seemed to slow down and speed up at the same time, shortly after the Maternal-Fetal Medicine Specialist's office scheduled us to come in and have another sonogram at their office.

When we arrived to the office that day, and was called back into the room. The nurse did the sonogram, showing us his heart, his little hands, feet, face, and his little manhood part, then cleaned Neshia back up. Before leaving she informed us that the doctor would be in to speak with us shortly. We sat down, not knowing what to really expect. Being that this was our first time and first child, we figure that this was nothing too major, and everything would eventually be okay. The doctor came into the room and seemed very pleasant. He shook both of our hands while introducing himself, before taking a seat directly in front of us. He asked how we were doing and did we know why we were there. We explained to him that the gynecologist had referred us there because they saw something on the sonogram that should be looked into further. The doctor then looks at both of us and says, "I have good news and bad news. Which one do you want first?" Of course you always want the good news first to kind of cushion the blow of the bad news, but before we could even answer, he then says, "I'll give you the bad news first!" The air in the room began to get thick with unease as that pleasant smile that we had in the beginning quickly started to fade into a stern look of worry. Neshia grabbed my hand, and pulled me closer to her. With my hand in hers he began to speak, *"Well, the baby's brain has not fully developed properly, which will cause serious complications in his development after he is born. When we looked at his brain on the sonogram, it appeared to be some empty spaces where his brain matter should have been".*

In the office, there were two large television screens on the wall behind him. He turns them both on. The screen on the left shows the sonogram of our son's brain, and the screen on the right shows what it should've looked like by the second trimester. He said to us with his little pointer thing pointed towards the right screen, *"Your brain is made up of two hemispheres that are divided in the center. However, with his case,"* pointing to our son's sonogram on the left screen, *"his brain never divided and the frontal lobe never developed".*

As he continued to explained to us what was going on, I glanced over at Neshia to see her reaction. Tears were flowing from her eyes like someone had turned on a water faucet. She clinched my hand tighter as if we were playing the game "Uncle". *"Most cases I've seen like this have resulted in babies being born with serious deformities or missing features, missing limbs, or even die shortly after birth,"* he says. *"Based upon the seriousness of his case, he will never be normal or have a normal life and neither will you guys either,"* explaining some of the difficulties that could arise. *"If you terminate the pregnancy, the good news is that by you guys being a very young couple, you can have another crack at it,"* he said, as if that was very encouraging."

Afterwards, the doctor left Neshia and I in the room for a moment, she laid on my shoulder and began to wail. I was speechless and in disbelief. I understood at that moment that my father was right! Before this moment, I had never suffered a day in my life. Eyes full of tears, my phone began to ring and guess who it was... it was my father. Ironic huh? *"Hello,"* I said; voice cracking, but trying to sound as normal as I could. *"Yeah son, what's going on,"* he said. I stepped out of the room into the hallway, because I didn't want Neshia to see me lose it. I began to explain to him exactly what the doctor explained to us. *"Well son,"* he says, *"It just gives God an opportunity to work a miracle for y'all."* He began to encourage me and remind me of what he told me prior, that this child would come through much prayer, but in the end, it was going to be okay, and everything would workout for God's glory. It was as though my father always knew exactly what to say to ease your mind about anything, and cause you to see the silver lining of every cloud. As he continued to encourage me, just that quick, my spirit was lifted a little, but yet my heart was still hurting. After speaking with my father, I went back in the room and sat back down next to Neshia. She looked at me and asked, *"Who was that on the phone?"* "That was Daddy," I said with a little smirk on my face. *"So, what did he say,"* probing me as she wiped her tears with her hand. "*He said everything's gonna be okay. God's gonna fix this,*" I told her as I laid her head on my shoulder. I think it comforted me more than her at the time.

The doctor entered the room again. As he sat down, he began asking us different questions concerning our medical history and our family's medical history. In my mind I believed this was is attempt to search for a probable cause behind this medical travesty. After the dreadful game of twenty-one questions had ended, he then scheduled us to have something called an amniocentesis procedure. Most women who have been through high risk pregnancy issues should know what an amniocentesis is. For those of you that don't know, an amniocentesis procedure is a prenatal test to examine the chromosomes of the fetus. The goal is to determine whether your unborn baby has any genetic abnormalities. The test is performed by sticking a long needle into the abdominal area to the amniotic sac to remove a sample of amniotic fluid for analysis. The results would determine whether or not there is a genetic disorder.

When we left the office that day, the car ride home seemed long and silent; no music from the radio or conversation, just silence. In the midst of that moment, I began to reflect back on everything that we had just experienced. I finally understood how

"I finally understood how one big moment; one minute of your life could ultimately change your whole life for the rest of your life."

one big moment in one single minute of your life could ultimately change your whole life- for the rest of your life. Neshia just sat there staring out the window; no words, just tears. And it was as though those silent tears that rolled down her face were louder than any cry that I had ever heard. Driving with tears rolling down my face as well, I was speechless. I had no words either. There were no encouraging words that I could even utter to help us cope with this, because the same pain and hurt that she felt, was the same pain and hurt that I felt. We just held each other's hand as if to say without saying, "I'm here. It's gonna be okay."

As we were driving home that day, my mind went to a familiar scripture concerning the prophet Elisha in 2nd Kings 4. Because Elisha the prophet would pass through their city frequently, a Shunammite woman and her husband decide to add a room onto their home for the prophet to stay and rest. Because of this, Elisha wanted to do something for them to show kindness and his gratitude. So he asked his servant, "How can we bless them?" The servant said to Elisha, "They don't have

What happens when the thing that you cherished the most bring to you the greatest heartbreak?

children." It was because this woman was barren. Then he prophesied to the Shunammite woman that she and her husband would have a son. Nine months later, that prophecy came to pass and they had a son. When their son had gotten a bit older, he went to work with his father, but then fell gravely ill. They then carried him to his mother, only to die on her lap later that day. She never called the funeral

home; she didn't begin making funeral plans, or even mention burying him. Instead, she laid him on the bed, in the room that they had built for the prophet when he came through the city. She saddled up and rode to see Elisha; that same prophet who interrupted her and her husband's life with something that had already

The Book of James

been settled in their minds that they would never experience; the same man who prophesied to them that they would bare a son. What happens when the thing that you cherished the most bring to you the greatest heartbreak?

Maybe a year or so prior, one of our real good friends in ministry; an awesome preacher and prophet came as a guest speaker at our church for our Wednesday night service. He calls Neshia and I up together to the front and said to us, "The Lord is about to bless you with a child. You're going to have a son, and this young child shall be a gift to you from God, because of the gift to God from you!" Never did we anticipate that we would receive a gift from God only for this heavenly gift to be delivered in a seemingly defective package! It just seemed so unfair. I called the prophet that had prophesied to us concerning us having a son. I told him about the situation and what the doctor had told us. Feeling disappointed, deceived, angry and heartbroken and just overcome with hurt, I became very irate on the phone. I began to blame him as if to say, "If you wouldn't have ever given us that flawed prophecy, Neshia and I would be fine right now. I just wanted to know why. Why was this happening to us? He could not answer my question. He was speechless and dumbfounded if I may say. I know now that it was God that hid from him the answer and therefore, he could not allow him to answer.

"For we know in part, and we prophesy in part."

2 Corinthians 13:9 KJV

This occurrence was almost as the prophet Elisha said in the passage when the Shunammite woman was coming down the street, and Elisha didn't know her reasoning for the visit. It wasn't a new moon neither the Sabbath.

"...her soul is vexed within her: and the LORD hath hid it from me, and hath not told me."

One morning as I was taking Neshia to work, we stopped in the drive-thru of Burger King to get breakfast. As we pulled up to the window to get the food, I can't remember exactly what song was playing on the radio before, but the next song that came on was Smokie Norful's song "I Need You Now." It was at that moment that the volcano of realization erupted. Neshia began to scream to the top of her voice, crying as though something or someone was literally hurting her. The people in the window were startled, looking, not knowing what was going on or in fact what to do. The girl in the window asked me, "*Is she okay?*" I shrugged my shoulders and shook my head yes, trying my best to hold back my tears, as I rubbed Neshia's back. I said to her, "*Yeah, we'll be okay.*"

The days following were filled with mixed emotions. We still had this gigantically heavy weight placed in our lap of whether or not to abort this child. This was a very difficult and painful decision because on one hand, we had been trying for a child for two years now. But on the other hand, we did not want a child that would not be normal, and would have to suffer with disabilities that would take away the quality of life for him as well as for us. We were still young, and still had a lot that we wanted to do in and with our lives. With both of us being raised in Christian homes, where our parents are pastors, abortion was not the likely option. I knew where my father stood in this. I never really talked about it much with my mother. She's a very quiet person and doesn't really give much input. My in-laws however, were much different in that regard. In talking with them, they explained to us, "*Ultimately, it's your decision. If you decide to terminate the pregnancy, it's okay. If you decide to go through with the pregnancy and have this child, it's going to be a lot of work, but we're here for you.*"

They understood first-hand the struggles of having to deal with disabilities and illnesses. Neshia's mother has been dealing with the sickle cell disease since her youth. Her mother's brother was disabled as well. But no matter how much we prayed or talked to our families about this, there was no easy answer.

Our faith was being tested in ways I could've never imagined. A few weeks past and the results from the amniocentesis were back. So we went back in to the office. The nurse came in to do the usual sonogram to check the status, growth, and development of the baby, and then told us that the doctor would be in to see us and give us the results from the amniocentesis shortly. As we sat there in the room quietly asking myself how much more of this bad news can we possibly take. I

"I really didn't want to hear anything else that would be devastating to us."

really didn't want to hear anything else that would be devastating to us. (As you can tell, I had now developed a phobia for doctor's offices.) The doctor entered the room and sat on the rolling stool. We went through all of the formalities, "Hey, how are you doing, etc." Then he said it again, *"Well, I've got good news and bad news. The good news is that the results of the amniocentesis procedure shows that genetically, the chromosomes are normal, and this was not a genetics issue. The bad news is that after studying his condition with a team of doctors, it is apparent that your son has a brain defect called Hōlō-prō-sen-cephaly."* I'm sure most of you don't have a clue what that is, or have never heard that word before. Trust me; it took me awhile to learn how to spell it. Holoprosencephaly is a relatively common birth defect of the brain, it often affects facial features, causing closely spaced eyes, small head size, and sometimes clefts of the lip and roof of the mouth. Not all with holoprosencephaly are affected to the same degree. It's characterized by the failure of the forebrain of the embryo to develop. During normal development, the forebrain is formed and the face begins to develop around the fifth and sixth weeks of pregnancy. Holoprosencephaly is caused by a failure of the embryo's forebrain to divide to form the left and right halves of the brain, causing developmental defects of the face and in brain structure.

At this point, in the doctors office, I'm completely numb. The doctor then says to us, *"Given that this child, your son, will have immediate complications, again, we strongly suggest that you consider terminating the pregnancy. Cases of this severity is proven to have devastating outcomes. However, we cannot make that decision for you. Go home; discuss this among yourselves, your family, your pastor or whomever you're comfortable with seeking advise from. Schedule a sit down with your gynecologist, and let them know how you want to proceed."*

After meeting with the gynecologist, who also suggest that we should terminate the pregnancy, after prayer and consulting with our parents, Neshia and I decided to keep the pregnancy. Because of our decision to go through with the birth of our son, we would have two to three doctor's appointments per week; from one doctor's office to the next; all still reminding us that at any time, if we decided to terminate this pregnancy, they could still do it.

Our last doctor visit was on Thursday, July 6th. At that appointment, the gynecologist went through his normal spill, and since we weren't budging on the termination of our son, anxious and exciting, we began discussing his arrival date. His actual due date was supposed to be on my birthday, which is July 26th, but because of his brain condition, the doctor did not want Neshia to go through a regular birth procedure, so they scheduled a cesarean section birth for July 13th.

On Thursday, July 13th at 5:00am, we got up, got dressed, and on our way to the hospital; anxious, excited, and a little frightened. When we got to the hospital, we checked in. They got her prepped and ready for delivery. This was a big moment for my family; the first grandchild for my parents, and the first nephew for my brothers. I waited in the waiting room with my family who all came to support this incredible moment. One of the nurses then walked in and called my name to follow her to the delivery room where Neshia was. When I got to the delivery room, right outside the room were all these specialists, and even the people from the morgue. Given the circumstances of his diagnosis, in the event that he was dead, they could rush him away quickly without us seeing him like that way.

***

Quad was born at 8:45am, weighing 5lbs 7oz. When the doctor delivered him, he had all of his facial features: eyes, nose, mouth, ears, and a head full of hair. His eyes were wide open, looking around. He was so alert. After they cleaned him off, suctioned him and wrapped him up in a blanket real good, they put him in my arms, and oh man, my heart skipped fifty beats. Our son; my namesake; James Brant IV; Quad; our miracle child; this awesome gift.

At that moment, while holding him and looking into his eyes, nothing else mattered. We forgot about everything the doctors and specialists had told us about his condition. He looked like a normal child. It was as though everything that the doctors had told us, God turned it around. Thank you Jesus. Hallelujah! Seems like that fairy tale happily ever after ending right? Nope; far from it!

"while holding him and looking into his eyes, nothing else mattered. We forgot about everything the doctors and specialists had told us about his condition."

A few days had passed since Quad's delivery, and we were still at the hospital. Neshia was healing from the cesarean section; not moving too much because of the staples. Of course, I was there trying to make her as comfortable as possible and running back and forth to see Quad and spend some early daddy-time with him. We were so excited about getting acclimated to having this new little life in our lives, having waited nine months for this; we were learning to feed him, burp him, change him.

One day, the doctor and one of the nurses came into the room to see us. While checking on Neshia's healing after the delivery the doctor began to give us an update on how our son Quad was doing. We thought it was going to be simple and end with date when we could all go home. Just as the doctor finishing examining her the ball dropped *"There is some issues with James' that we're kind of concerned about,"* he said. *"During his feeding times, while eating he stops breathing, which makes it difficult for him to eat and breathe simultaneously."* I stood still and tried to remember how to breathe as her continued talking. *"Given that he has been previously diagnosed with Holoprosencephaly, that may be an area of his brain that is presenting this complication. After delivery, we ran more tests, CT scan, sonograms, and x-rays, etc. We discovered that James has only one kidney, and strangely, his heart has uniquely developed faced down, and his right pulmonary artery was not developed. So we need to do surgery to construct that right artery or he could later be in danger of losing a lung,"* he explained to us. *"We are going to have to transfer him over to the Newborn Intensive Care Unit (NICU) at Wolfson Children's Hospital for the surgery and further observation,"* he said. Neshia sat up in the bed with this unexplainable look on her face. It was almost like that look of "I'm not understanding what you're saying," compiled with the

> *"All of the joy and exuberance that we felt when our son entered this world was just vacuumed out like dirt out of a rug."*

look of "You gotta be kidding me right now." All of the joy and exuberance that we felt when our son entered this world was just vacuumed out like dirt out of a rug. I was empty! After a few seconds passed he continued to speak *"As for the flipping of his heart,"* he said, *"because it's beating at the normal rate, we'll leave it alone."* He comes over and stands between Neshia and I to offer a hug to us both. With a little smile on his face and says, *"We love with our heart faced upward; let's see how he loves with his faced downward."* At this point, we're thrown for a loop, because not only have they diagnosed our son with Holoprosencephaly, now we find out that he is born with only one kidney and has to go through open heart surgery. So Quad was transferred from St. Vincent's Medical Center, (where he was born) to the NICU at Wolfson Children's Hospital.

For the most part of this chapter, I have talked about me and my thoughts and how I felt. But one day I remembered Neshia and I were just laying in the bed at home, and tears began to roll down her face. She laid her head on my chest and said, *"Why did all of this happen to us? What did we do so wrong for this to happen to us? Why would God do this to us? I don't understand. We did it right! We waited until we got married. Others have had children out of wedlock, and some with multiple people, but they have healthy children. Why would God do this to us?"* She began to go back in her mind, examining her life and both our lives to find something that we may have done wrong that may have caused this to happen as a result. And at that moment, here comes John 9 in my mind again. In that scripture, here was a young man blind from birth; his parents probably wondered within themselves because of their belief, "We must've done something to cause this misfortune on our son?" And because of this impairment, believe it or not, this young man would probably need assistance most, if not all of his life, which makes it not only a challenge for him, but also for his parents who were constantly reminded that there was a possibility that this was the result of something that they did or did not do. Being just as hurt and confused as she was and having asked God the same questions in my own mind, but now attempting to comfort her as much as I could, I said to her, *"Baby, we didn't do anything wrong. This wasn't our fault."* I then reminded her of the story in John 9, and how it was neither the man's fault nor his parents, but that there was a miracle that Jesus wanted to show everybody that day. Husbands, listen to me carefully. This is why it is so important that we take our roles as being the priests of our homes, because God will use His priests as His mouthpiece to bring peace! (I know that just rhymed, but it's powerful.)

So, comparing John 9 to our situation, there's not much of a difference. Here are parents that are given a son, which represents the favor of God in a family, but the favor is faulty! So if not their fault, then whose fault is this? Who is to blame for this? Jesus speaks to the disciples in the 3rd verse and silences their inquisitive conclusions. It finally hit me: this really had nothing to do with Neshia and I.

Let's do a quick review: After the amniocentesis procedure, the results determined that our genetics were fine. There were no chromosome issues. He was born with only one kidney, and less than two weeks old, he undergoes an open heart surgical procedure. Later on, they determined that the chromosome that should have suggested that he has Holoprosencephaly, there is no trace of it; yet he has Holoprosencephaly. The team of doctors who studied my son's condition equated that this had to have been just a fluke of nature, but John 9:3 suggests that this was done to manifest the glory of God in him. What do you think?

2

A New Kind of Normal

(The Paradigm Shift)

[12] I know both how to be abased, and I know how to abound:
every where and in all things I am instructed both to be full and
to be hungry, both to abound and to suffer need. [13] I can do all
things through Christ which strengthens me.
Philippians 4:12-13 KJV

Paradigm shift is defined as a dramatic change in methodology and practice. It often refers to major changes in thinking and planning, which ultimately alters the way things are implemented. For example: years ago, there were Polaroid cameras. In those days, the film had to be developed in a darkroom, which the developing process itself took a few days. Extracting the film from a camera, it was then taken in the darkroom where the negatives from the film are produced. The negatives are

"Paradigm shift...forces you to adapt to its terms without any debate, discussion, compromise, or even agreement."

placed in a solution that help to develop the picture. Now, we have iPhones, smart phones, iPads and tablets where you can take pictures and instantly view and edit the picture taken yourself.

Another example: years ago, to send and/or receive information from one person or place to another, there was facsimile or fax. It was a big thing to have a fax machine back in the day. The fax machine used a special type of paper that came on a roll, similar to receipt paper from a cash register. So given the fax machine used a special type of paper and not just regular letter size paper, what would happen then if you ran out of paper, and you're waiting for an important message? You couldn't feed regular paper into the fax machine back then. Now we have electronic mail or email, where you can send and/or receive information in seconds over the world wide web with just a few clicks of a button. And because of this technological paradigm shift, and with almost everyone in the world having an email address, the email era has rendered fax almost obsolete these days.

We are all at some point or another in our life victims of paradigm shifts. One of the most uncomfortable things about a paradigm shift is that it renders you totally helpless against it, and there is no other alternative but to roll with the punches; adapt and adjust. Change is never comfortable, however, sometimes it is very needful, but most of all, change is inevitable. It forces you to adapt to its terms without any debate, discussion, compromise, or even agreement.

This chapter is a little fast forwarded view of the dramatic shift that took place in our lives; a paradigm shift that would forever change us to the point that it would almost erase the moments and memories of how it used to be before this shift occurred. This may help someone: when you can embrace the shift, you can then adapt to the shift, and what others have equated to be impossible for them to handle has become a new normal for you.

Most times our prayer is "Lord, deliver me out of this," instead of "Lord, develop me in this." I believe this statement arises from an immature state of mind, because we don't understand the power of those catastrophes, and how they transfer virtue to us. It gives to you an exchange, but not only that; it equips you with a special gift that before that exchange, you didn't have.

"Paradigm shift...forces you to adapt to its terms without any debate, discussion, compromise, or even agreement."

So many people come to Neshia and I after seeing how well we care for Quad. (We keep him fashion forward and super fresh every day; everything is always in place;) Most people ask the same question, "How do y'all do it?" Listen, it's not easy at all! There have been so many things that we have had to rearrange, subtract, add, divide, and multiply in and from our lives in order to survive this paradigm shift. We both ended up or should I say, we were FORCED to quit our jobs to take care of the needs of our son. She had an amazing job at Florida Retina Institute making good money. I was employed at Florida Metropolitan University, a career college. I was there almost six years, making great money with awesome benefits and perks .

I do believe that God has a very unique sense of humor, all the while most times it's not that funny to us; we're not laughing. In fact, at times we're crying, suffering, and sometimes we feel as though we're alone; at least for the moment that's what we think is going on. However, truthfully speaking, we are just going through the developing process.

Even now as I'm writing I'm looking at my son sitting in his chair. Sometimes I wonder to myself, "How does he feel about his life? Does he feel like he has been robbed of any qualities of life? What is his greatest frustration? What is he thinking right now?" Of course, there are many other questions I have and other things I wonder about, and hopefully one day soon, he'll be able to communicate with us what is really going on in that little head of his. Now back to the question " How do we do it?"

People come up to us all the time and commend us for being good young parents, and hanging in there despite the cards dealt to us. They often want to know how are we able to do all that we do ministry, work, traveling, etc., yet Quad is never neglected, and still has the greatest quality of life; nothing lacking. I believe Neshia would agree with me when I say, "My father." When Quad was born, with all the situations surrounding his condition, and having gone through that surgery, and having to be on constant care, we were forced to quit our jobs. My father stepped in and hired me to work full-time at our church. I became the chaplain of our Christian Academy as well as the executive pastor and administrator for our church. This gave me flexibility to work on salary and also still be available for my son at moment's notice if need be.

Truth be told, I had been praying to the Lord that entire year my desire to work full-time in ministry, not knowing that God's timing was about to manifest just that. Quad was born on July 13th, and my last day working for Florida Metropolitan University was December 31st of the same year.

I was hired by my father and started working full-time at the church seven days later. Neshia began teaching Kindergarten and first grade at the school in August of the same year, which was actually the following school year. Now both of us are working in full-time in the ministry and have been now for twelve years.

"I had been praying to the Lord that entire year my desire to work full-time in ministry, not knowing that God's timing was about to manifest..."

Everyday is not one of perfection, but we have really gotten good at this thing. Honestly, everyday has a bit of a learning curve in it. We have discovered that our lives are not at all complicated, but rather complexed, and there is a vast difference between the two. Many times these two words are mistakenly used to be seemingly interchangeable, but they are different and that difference makes a difference. So what then is the difference between being complicated and complexed?

To be complex refers to the number of components in a system. So if a problem is complexed, it means that it has many different components or compartments. Complexity does not necessarily cause difficulty. The problem may be simple, however, because of its multiple components or compartments, it may just be more time consuming. But being complicated on the other hand, refers to a high level of difficulty. So if the problem is complicated, it means that there may or may not necessarily be many components, and there may or may not even be a solution to that problem.

Quad added complexity to our lives as well as flexibility; a lot of complexity and a lot of flexibility. There are many facets from the time he gets up in the morning until he's put to bed that have to be executed for that day to be a success one. Here are some of the basic medicines that he takes daily; not including the times he gets sick, just the everyday stuff. Are you ready? Here we go…

Pulmicort Respules: an anti-inflammatory steroid used to prevent asthma attacks, hay fever and other allergies. He has to have this medicine through his nebulizer in the morning and the evening.

Albuterol: prevents and treats wheezing, shortness of breath, coughing, and chest tightness. It relaxes and opens the air passages to the lungs to make his breathing easier. This medicine is administered through the nebulizer as well, only in the evening.

Diazepam: also known as Valium and is used for extreme muscle spasms and anxiety. He gets 2mg three times a day.

Cuvposa: help to reduce his chronic severe drooling. He gets 5ml three times a day.

Ranitidine: used to prevent ulcers in the stomach and intestines and treats acid reflux. He gets 15ml once daily when he wakes up.

Hydrocortisone _(Cortef)_: a corticosteroid used to treat low cortisol levels; important for salt and water balance and keeping his blood pressure normal. He has to have this three times a day: 5mg in the morning, 2.5mg in the afternoon, and 2.5mg in the evening.

Probiotic: a natural supplement that helps to support his immune and digestive system. It restores the natural balance of good bacteria in the digestive tract. He takes this once a day.

Levothyroxine: thyroid medicine that replaces a hormone normally produced by your thyroid gland to regulate the body's energy and also the metabolism. Levothyroxine is given when the thyroid does not produce enough of this hormone on its own. Levothyroxine treats hypothyroidism (low thyroid hormone). He gets ½ tablet once a day in the evening.

Elderberry: natural supplement used to boost the immune system. He gets 10ml once a day in the evening as well.

Claritin: an antihistamine that reduces the effects of natural histamine in the body. It reduces sneezing, itching, watery eyes, and runny nose. He takes 10ml once daily.

Singulair _(Montelukast)_: a 5mg tablet used as a maintenance treatment for asthma, taken once daily. He gets this in the morning when he wakes up.

Patanase Nasal Spray: relieves symptoms of seasonal allergies that occur such as stuffy nose and post nasal drip. He takes this at bedtime.

Zyrtec: used to treat allergy symptoms. He takes 10ml daily.

Motrin/Ibuprofen: an anti-inflammatory drug used to treat pain , 15ml taken twice per day.

Intrathecal Baclofen Pump: a surgically implanted system used to control spasticity by infusing liquid Baclofen directly into the spinal canal and around the spinal cord.

G-tube Feeding Pump: a gastronomy feeding tube is inserted through the skin into the stomach wall. Because he is unable to eat or drink by mouth, all of his nutrition and medicines are given through his G-tube.

SmartVest Airway Clearance System: a high frequency chest wall oscillation powered by a portable air-pulse generator; used to break up mucus from the lungs and clear the airway. This treatment is for 45 minutes in the morning and 45 minutes in the evening.

He also takes other medicine as needed such as: Valium and Baclofen for sudden dystonia spells.

***

Quad is twelve years old and he's now in the sixth grade at an exceptional educational institution. He also receives his physical, occupational, and speech therapy. Even after twelve years we are still adjusting to the new normal. Work begins for us at 7:45am, so it's imperative that everyone's clothes are ironed,

"Yeah, I know! Your head is already spinning. Trust me, our heads were spinning at first too."

showers, etc. are done the night before. Planning ahead and being flexible has been our saving grace because Quad depends on us for everything. His overnight PediaSure milk feeding begins at 10:00pm.

He gets 475-500ml at a rate of 71ml per hour. Our 6:00am alarm goes off, which is his feeding pump. He then has to be changed and given all of his morning medicines (Singulair, Hydrocortisone, Diazepam, Cuvposa, Ranitidine, Gabapentin, Motrin/Ibuprofen, and 20ml of water). He has to be on his SmartVest no later than 6:10am, because the SmartVest treatment alone takes forty-five minutes and his school bus comes at 7:25am. It would seem logical to just get up earlier right? Wrong! He has to have all of his calories from the overnight feed, because he was diagnosed with "Failure to Thrive," which causes his calorie intake to have to be monitored. Yeah, I know! Your head is already spinning. Trust me, our heads were spinning at first too.

While he's on the SmartVest treatment, we also give him his Albuterol and Pulmicort nebulizer treatments simultaneously, but separately. This gives us fifteen minutes extra for me to get dressed while Neshia finishes drawing up his other medicines for the day. After both treatments are done, Quad needs to be changed again, lotioned, and then his clothes and shoes put on. Here's the funny thing: he never wants Neshia to put his clothes on. He really gives her a hard time. So I'm responsible for getting him dressed every morning. Next, his teeth have to be brushed, strapped into his wheelchair, daily backpack ready, hair brushed, and on the bus. Now we have maybe only fifteen minutes left to finish getting dressed and out the door. Between 6:00am and 7:45am, it seems as though an hour and forty-five minutes is in fact an entire day. After all of that, just to get the day started, I'm sure all of you would love to just get back in the bed. So by 7:45am, our day is well on its way.

Quad gets out of school at 3:00pm. So 3:40-4:00pm, his bus drops him off. By this time, his 2:00pm PediaSure feed is done. His first PediaSure feed of the day is at 10:00am. At 11:30am, he gets his first dose of baclofen. That's the only medicine he gets at school aside from his Albuterol treatment, and also he gets flushed with 200ml of water at 12:45pm.

When Quad gets home, he has to have his 3:00pm medicines (Diazepam, Hydrocortisone, Zyrtec, Gabapentin, Cuvposa, and Motrin/Ibuprofen). He probably has to also be changed again, and then given his forty-five minute SmartVest treatment. After his treatment, he gets his 4:45pm flush of water. By this time, Quad is exhausted from school and usually takes a long nap, because he's very nosey and doesn't take a nap during nap time. His flush is usually done between 5:15pm and 5:25pm. His next PediaSure feed isn't until 6:00pm. So we give him his bath between that time, because his PediaSure feeds last about an hour and thirty minutes, and it's important to capitalize on every minute. After Quad is bathed and right before his feed time, he gets his 6:00pm medicines (Probiotic, Baclofen, Elderberry, and Motrin/Ibuprofen).

After the 6:00pm feed begins the preparation cycle of ironing, and organizing for the next day begins again . He also gets his nebulizer treatment (Pulmicort and Albuterol), the Patanase nasal spray, his 8:45pm medicine (Levothyroxine), flush and off to bed. Generally, by his 10:00pm overnight feed and evening medicines (Gabapentin, Cuvposa, Hydrocortisone, and Diazepam), Quad is out; only to start all over again tomorrow. Now, that's just the typical day in our house. The truth is, there are not many days in our house that will go that smoothly. That wasn't a church night or a doctor's appointment day! Sometimes things can go way left field, but we have to conform to whatever shift may take place that day and make it work.

About a year ago I was asked if Neshia and I ever had a real vacation-just the two of us. Of course some of you already know my response to that…NO! There simply is no way because of the needs of our son. My father was the senior pastor and presiding bishop of an international organization and another fellowship as well. My mother was always right by his side and they're always out of town; sometimes at moments notice. So their schedule was always…, well you know. All of my siblings have families of their own. Neshia's parents would love to keep him for us sometime, and they do but not overnight. Due to her mother's sickness, they're not able to, which we totally understand. And Quad is not a baby anymore. This dude is over 70lbs now, and that's not actually an easy task. We have tried applying for a stay-at-home nurse through his insurance, but didn't qualify. We don't make enough yet to hire a part-time nanny; them knowing how to draw up all of his medicines; when his feeding and flushing times are; when to do this; when to do that......, and even finding someone that we can trust with him considering the world that we're living in now, it's rough, nearly impossible. So Quad's situation requires that we do almost everything together. Dates? Yes, we do go on dates. Consequently, it's the three of us. Movies? We go to the movies. And yes, it's the three of us. We have also gone to the beach. We haven't been in awhile, but of course, it was the three of us; Quad's wheelchair and all. A getaway trip for us could never be a getaway, because a getaway trip for us would only be based upon changing locations, but never changing the situation.

***

Listen, I know this can be so upsetting and very discouraging to many married couples and maybe even you, the reader. I guess to the average person, this would be detrimental to a marriage or relationship, not having time alone to spend with your significant other to invest in your relationship, and getting away for rest, relaxation, and resort. And to an extent, that maybe true. Those are things that are honestly the essential heartbeat of a healthy relationship. There are many couples today that force themselves to live or remain in certain dysfunctional situations solely for the sake of their children. They will co-exist, and live under a miserably false pretense to keep the appearance of a sense of togetherness and balance for the child or children. However, it will later present a multiplicity of other issues that may not be very visual per say, but more unconsciously influential.

So with our case, we have had to create space and opportunities for those things in our marriage and relationship to occur. We do engage in deep and intimate conversations riding along in the car, or pillow talk at night, of course after Quad goes to bed. Sometimes we even end up falling asleep in the middle of conversations because we're so tired. We still like flirting through text messages throughout the day while at work, to kind of keep the spice alive. And because we work at the church and the school, we're on the same campus, sometimes I'll go over to her classroom on my break, or she'll come over to my office on her break.

" We intentionally make affectionate gestures apparent to Quad at home, because it's important for him to see ."

We intentionally make affectionate gestures apparent to Quad at home, because it's important for him to see mommy and daddy hug and kiss, laugh, play, and have fun with each other at home. We have really managed to fit our relationship into our situation. I guess you can call it a "SITUATION-SHIP." So living a new kind of normal is all based upon how you view it; your perspective.

Now I'm sure all of us by now have heard of optical illusion. If you haven't, indulge me for a moment. Optical illusion is information through an image that is gathered by the eye, and processed in the brain to see the image in a way that is different from how the image appears. *(See the image below)*

Is it a duck or a rabbit? The truth is that there is no right or wrong answer, because your answer that you give is based solely upon your perspective and how you see the image. Optical illusions provides one image with multiple perspectives, and what you see is sometimes based upon how long you look at it.

In the gospel of Matthew chapter 16, Jesus gives an incredible lesson on the power of perspective. He asked his disciples the question, *"Whom do men say that I the son of man am?"* And they began to tell Jesus what others were saying about Him, and who others thought Him to be. Jesus then directs the question from another angle, *"But whom say ye that I am?"* One man, different perspectives. Others on the outside had their perspective, and their perspective was based upon the time spent with Him. His disciples however, walked with Him daily and had a deeper relationship with Him. Therefore, because of the quantity of time invested, their views were different.

In my conclusion, my point is this: How do you see what you see when you look at where you are from where you are? Is the glass half empty or half full? It is simply all in how you look at it!

14 And they said, Some say that thou art John the Baptist: some, Elias; and others, Jeremias, or one of the prophets. 15 He saith unto them, But whom say ye that I am?

Matthew 16:14-15

3

Impression... The Aftermath

(The Blah Moments)

"Then I said, I will not make mention of him, nor speak any more in his name. But his word was in mine heart as fire shut in my bones..."

Jeremiah 20:9 KJV

I have not always felt like this about everything that has happened in my life. I don't have the testimony that through it all, I never wavered in my faith or my trust in God. In the previous chapter, we talked about a paradigm shift, and how it ultimately force you to adapt to its terms. This chapter is my more candid and transparent view of the paradigm shift. Listen clearly and carefully; it's not always about what happens in life, but rather how what happens in life affect us afterward; the aftermath, which can have an effect on how we cope with things internally, although possibly masking it externally. There are some situations that occur in our lives that can leave us with very deep scars; scars that may not always be visibly seen on the outside, but sometimes may cause us to react based upon the impression that that scar has left inside as a result.

There is a difference between impact and impression. These two words are most times used interchangeably; however, they are similar in interaction, but different in experience.

Impact

To impact something or someone is to have a direct effect on or to strike with great force. For instance: two vehicles collide, WHAM! The force from the collision has now effected the outer structure of both vehicles. Following impact, one of two chain of events can erase any trace that the impact of the collision ever occurred. One: they can get another vehicle; same year, make, model, and color. Or two: they can hire a collision body repair shop to restore the vehicle to its original form and color. Both can erase any evidence that the vehicle had been in a collision.

Impression

Impression however, is somewhat different, because it is defined as favorable influence or an effect on your feelings, senses, and even your mind.

When I was about four years old, there was a lamp in my room that fell off of the corner of the dresser. This lamp had no lamp shade on it. When the lamp fell off the dresser, it touched my right arm. The bulb was so hot that it literally burnt my skin. I am now thirty-nine years old, and that scar is still there today. It's not as visible today as it was then, but it's still there.

However, because of that catastrophic experience as a four-year-old little boy, as a thirty-nine-year-old man, I refuse to change a light bulb unless the light switch is off or the lamp is unplugged. In fact,

Impression…effect was more interior, whereas an impact is more exterior.

every time I look at my right forearm, I can remember almost everything about that occurrence that day. That incident left an impression; an indelible mark not only on my right forearm, but in my mind that could never be erased. Its effect was more interior, whereas an impact is more exterior.

***

Shortly after Quad was born, after the surgery and being released from the hospital, as new parents, we were still in denial that there was anything wrong with our son. Of course, he was a newborn; there's not much you can really see at this point. And nobody wants to accept that there is or could possibly be something wrong with your child. Our denial lasted awhile, and then Neshia began to notice little things that Quad should've been doing by now that he wasn't doing. It became difficult for him to swallow at feeding times, and he would not hold his bottle. We just assumed that he was being stubborn and didn't want the bottle. But then, we began to notice that he wasn't finishing a full 6oz bottle. At the end of a day, he would still have almost 4oz left. By this time, Quad was a little over six months. He was not sitting up unsupported, rolling over, reaching or holding things, propping himself up, and was well under the weight that he should've been as a six-month old child.

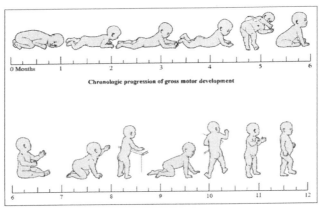

We were given a chart *(similar to the image above)* that would show us what his normal development and progression should be. It also described some of the activities that he should have by now been engaging curiosity toward. And his weight was well below the average child. So we scheduled to see a nutritionist to get a better understanding of what's going on with and why he was not finishing his bottles. They scheduled a swallow study on him and discovered that due to the diagnosis of Holoprosencephaly, his ability to swallow had been affected, which therefore, he was further diagnosed with failure to thrive.

For those of you who have never heard the term "Failure to Thrive," it is when a child's weight is significantly lower or below that of other children of similar age. So after having diagnosed him, they began to talk to us about inserting a feeding tube into his stomach, because his ability to eat or drink by mouth was diminishing. We agreed to the procedure, and he had the feeding tube surgically inserted. Now, he would get most of his nutrition, if not all, through his feeding tube. People, this was really not going good for us; well, let me say it wasn't going good for me. To think, here we are, by this time, one of my brothers have children and another has a child on the way; healthy children, but Neshia and I were struggling to do all we could to keep our baby alive. I'm began to slowly sink into a place where the light was quickly dimming. My view was narrowing and I felt myself losing sight on everything else around me. We prayed! We were prayed for. We ran to the scriptures for encouragement. I kept preaching and leading people in worship into the presence of the Lord, but after awhile, I became numb. I preached because that's what I was supposed to do; that's what I've been called to do, but at the same time, I didn't feel anything.

"I preached because that's what I'm supposed to do; that's what I've been called to do, but at the same time, I didn't feel anything."

I led the congregation in praise and worship week in and week out, but eventually, I didn't feel anything anymore. Most of (if not everything) the things I was doing became solely based upon "know-how." Let's not forget, I'm a PK *(Preacher's Kid)*. I was born and raised in the church. So it's not hard to just "do church." It's second nature to us! I believe that every PK that will read this book can agree with me that if our parents ever left the church in our hands for one service… We know how to everything; pray, sing, preach, take up the offering, baptize, etc. And it has nothing to do with being saved; it's just cultural rehearsal and redundancy. And guess what? We can do it without relationship.

In the book of 1 Samuel 3, the Bible said that when Samuel was a young child, he ministered unto the Lord before Eli. Eli taught Samuel all of the duties of the priesthood, ceremonies and rituals of the temple, yet without relationship. He knew how to do "church" and that where I was at the time. I began to feel as though I was losing it and God really didn't even care.

When Neshia told me that she was pregnant again, oh the joy that flooded my soul! There was a freedom that came over me that was unexplainable; freedom from this feeling of unfair treatment, defeat, frustration, helplessness and emptiness; a burden had just been lifted from my shoulders. At that moment, I knew that this next child would be, not a replacement of Quad, but compensation for what we had gone through, even as God gave Adam and Eve Seth as compensation for the death of Abel. I was so excited, overwhelmed, and assured that God had not forgotten us. We kept the announcement of the pregnancy under wraps, because we did not want to jinx anything by spilling the beans prematurely and not even make it past the first trimester. We went to the doctor, and they confirmed that there was indeed a little bun in the oven. She was only a few weeks, however, there was a strong heartbeat.

On April 20, 2009, my brother's beautiful little daughter Jayde was born, and we were on the way out to the hospital to see her and congratulate my brother. On our way there, we saw Neshia's youngest brother Randy walking. We pulled over and chatted with him for a few minutes, and then off to see our new little niece. We got to the hospital and saw little Jayde, and talked with the rest of the family, laughing and having fun.

After getting home and getting Quad settled and asleep, we went to bed. Around 4:00am the next morning, Neshia's phone rang. She answers the phone, "Hello," with that real sleepy voice. I'm usually not really a heavy sleeper, so I can hear the whole conversation. It was her mother. "He's gone Neshia; he's dead!" "Mama, who," Neshia said, rolling over toward me, stretching. "Randy! He's dead Neshia," her mother screaming hysterically. We had just talked to Randy, not even twelve hours ago, and now he's gone?

We jumped up and got dressed. We got Quad up and got him dressed as well. I called my father and told him what had happened, and he agreed to meet us at the hospital.

When we got to the hospital, they directed us to the back where he was. My mother-in-law and father-in-law were standing by Randy's body, one holding his hand, and the other, rubbing the side of his face. His body was still warm. *" It was her mother. "He's gone Neshia; he's dead!" "Mama, who..."* We were so devastated beyond words! Randy was only twenty-four years old and healthy; he just died. Neshia and I had been together, or as the young people call it, "going out" since Randy was in elementary. He was not just my brother-in-law; he was my brother. That week was a very trying week for both our families, because for so long, our families had been so closely knitted together.

The day after laying Randy to rest, Neshia's mother had a sickle cell crisis from the stress of the loss and was hospitalized. Two days later, Quad was admitted into the hospital for pneumonia. It was an overly stressful time; so much until Neshia's stomach began to swell abnormally. She was only about twelve weeks, but her stomach within days began to grow as though she was six or seven months. We knew something just wasn't right! We immediately called and made an appointment to see the doctor.

When we got to the doctor's office, of course you have to do all of the preliminaries; sign in, record your weight and the growth of the belly, etc. They then put us in one of the rooms to wait for the doctor. The doctor came in and greeted us as he always does, and said, *"Your stomach has really grown since the last time we saw you. That's not normal, but lets have a look."* They set her up on the table and squirted the gel on her stomach, preparing to do the ultrasound. While doing the ultrasound, we were just chatting and shooting the breeze. After all, this was the same doctor that we had when she was pregnant with Quad. He then shows us the screen and says, *"You have an abnormal amount of fluid in there, which is the reason why your stomach is so big. It took a while to find it, but I did. There are two in there; twins. Unfortunately, there were no heartbeats. Mr. and Mrs. Brant, I'm really sorry for your loss. I know how much this really meant for you all to try again."* It was believed that the high level of stress from the death of Neshia's youngest brother, the hospitalization of both her mother and Quad was way too much for her to handle and for the twins to survive. Twins!

The doctor walked out of the room, and gave us a little time to get ourselves together after the news. Neshia began to cry, and I grabbed and held her very tight, so tight that air couldn't *" the hospitalization of both her mother and Quad was way too much for her to handle and for the twins to survive"* pass between the both of us. I've had this feeling before. I knew it all too well. It was all too familiar, and never once did I think or fathom that we would ever be reacquainted with this most dreadful occurrence again in life. There we were again sitting with me hold her with helpless arms. We were in the midst of yet another hopeless situation, with both our hearts now seemingly unsalvageable.

The doctor came back in the room with one of his assistance. After expressing again his sympathy, he began to discuss with us the next process called

Dilation and Curettage or D&C. Dilation and Curettage is a surgical procedure that is performed after a first trimester miscarriage. They would dilate the cervix and extract the expired fetuses from the uterus. The procedure was scheduled and performed within the next four days. As the healing process of Neshia's body began after the procedure, her mind seemingly headed in the opposite direction. Questions no one could answer; questions only a mother would have lingering in the back of her mind for years to come; thinking and believing that she was a cursed human being and asking *"Why would God allow me to conceive twins and to feel them move inside my womb, only to never see their beautiful faces; contemplating who they would favor or have traits like; mommy or daddy?"*

We were so distraught and broken. It was as if we were characters in a horror movie unbeknownst to our consent. However, there were no cameras. There was no script; no lighting engineer; no props and no director on the set. There were no stunt doubles, producers, audio technicians, or wardrobe designer, and we certainly wasn't getting paid for this. This was far from acting. No, this was no act; this was reality!

As a husband, this is a very hard and devastating blow to a man's ego, because of his nature and how God made him, he feels as though he's suppose to have all the answers to that wife's

" As a husband, this is a very hard and devastating blow to a man's ego... "

questions. Listen to me: "MAN" is the acronym for "<u>M</u>eet <u>A</u>ll <u>N</u>eeds." He's supposed to know how to fix the problem. He's supposed to be her Superman, and swoop in and save the day. He's supposed to possess the arms of security and safety that protects her from harm. After all, he vowed to love, honor, and protect her; protecting her from anything or anybody. And I was so prepared to protect her, even if it meant standing up to God himself on her behalf.

The cry that I heard that day from her, was like no other cry I had ever heard before. Heartbreak, agony, pain, and disappointment were the ingredients in this cry. And because of this cry and the pain that we have dealt with, not only from the miscarriage, but also from the grief of the loss of her brother, the stress of her mother being in the hospital, Quad's hospitalization and his ongoing situations, I became extremely pissed with God. Okay, I know I know; some of you can't agree with me on that one. *"God is too wise to make a mistake, and He's too just to do wrong;"* another church cliché! Let me help you understand something: as saved and as Holy Ghost filled as you think you are, there are things that can happen in your life that are so detrimental that can affect you internally, and as a result, your response or reaction externally becomes an evident reflection of your internal impression.

I called my mother and told her what had happened and what the doctor said. She said to me, "Well, you need to call your daddy and tell him what's going on." "Nope," I said. *"That's alright! I don't want to hear another scripture; I don't want hear another sermon; I don't want anymore prayer. I am done. God cannot be as real as we say he is to allow this to happen to us again,"* walking out of the hospital with tears lapped under my chin. *"I'm through. This is it! Preaching, singing, playing; all of it; I'm done."* After hanging up the phone with my mother, I was standing on the outside of the hospital and I began to tell God

" your response or reaction externally becomes an evident reflection of your internal impression "

off with everything in me. *"I've played, sang, preached, tithed, given, offered my life to your service, and you do this to us? My wife doesn't deserve this, God. This is the second time you've done this to us, but I won't wait around for a third; I'm done with you!"* And in that moment, I meant every word! I can hear some of you right now saying, "You're lucky you ain't dead; talking to God like that." In all honesty, I believe that God gives us the opportunity to be human. Even in our humanness he knows that the "YES" He's placed in us from the beginning-before the foundations of the world, is so much greater than the "NO" of our present day circumstances.

Then the word of the LORD came unto me saying, Before I formed thee in the belly, I knew thee; and before thou camest forth out of the womb I sanctified thee, and I ordained thee a prophet to the nations. Then said I, Ah Lord GOD! Behold, I cannot speak: for I am a child. But the LORD said unto me, Say not, I am a child: for thou shalt go to all that I shall send thee, and whatsoever I command thee thou shalt speak.

Jeremiah 1:4-7 KJV

There was another instance where Jeremiah's present circumstance attempted to alter his answer concerning his destiny. He was imprisoned, devastated, and disappointed, but his "YES" prevailed.

God doesn't wait until you're born to orchestrate your life. This "YES" that you gave God was consented by you long before you ever entered time. Our present "NO" has no ability or weight to breach the contract of the conversation of consent in eternity, before you got here.

" God doesn't wait until you're born to orchestrate your life. "

The next few years after losing the twins were pretty blah! I don't remember much at all. Yeah, I was still going to church. I was still preaching, playing, and singing, but the pain and the bitterness was still there so immense that I think I place myself under a mental and psychological anesthesia, and blocked out some of those years. Sound crazy huh? Most of the things during that time span I really don't remember. One of the lasting memories of my son's birthday was his first birthday party. Everything after that is kind of blurry and I can't remember exactly. Trips, getaways, family outings, if there were any; photo shoots, special occasions, I don't really remember. Neshia was very good at taking lots of pictures of everything that we had done together as a family. They were all downloaded onto my MacBook. So at any time, to be reminded of things that we had done as a family, I could get my MacBook and pull them up.

One day my MacBook was stolen, and it really rocked my world. That small electronic device had my world on it. I was also a graphic designer as well as all that other stuff you know about me. Graphic designing was my little side business or side hustle, if you will. So with my MacBook being stolen, all of my clients' files, artwork, logos, flyers, websites, and even a few opened contracted client's work that I was finishing up were gone. My recording album masters, school files, church files; everything was gone! Man, I was so angry! How will I ever be able to recreate these files, and all of these things that I've accumulated over the years? The clients that I had opened contracts with; I had to refund them their deposits and refer them to someone else until I could regroup, and put things back together again.

It wasn't until months later that I realized all of the pictures that we had taken since Quad's birth well were gone. All of the memorable moments, trips, daycare, kindergarten graduation; everything that had proven itself to be a memory crutch for me was gone! Tell me, what do you do when the crutch that you've designed to justify your reasoning for immaturity now breaks? It wasn't until that moment that I really had to wake up, realize, and understand that despite my anger and bitterness toward God, I was also causing my son to have to live

and experience the life of a child who is parented by an absent father who has been present every day. Oxymoronic huh? But, the light bulb really came on y'all. I became angrier with myself than with God. In being angry with God, I began deflecting the effects of my pain, anger, and bitterness toward my son who was already experiencing enough challenges of his own…

"What do you do when the crutch that you've designed to justify your reasoning for immaturity now breaks?"

Then I said, I will not mention of him, nor speak any more of his name. But his word was in mine heart as a burning fire shut up in my bones, and I was weary with forbearing, and I could not stay.

Jeremiah 20:9 KJV

The Necessity of Pain

(Finding Purpose In Pain)

"For I know the thoughts that I think toward you, saith the Lord, thoughts of peace, and not of evil, to give you an expected end."

Jeremiah 29:11 KJV

The apostle Paul, in his second letter to the Corinthian church *(2 Corinthians 12),* speaks about a very troubling point in his life; that ultimately proved extremely beneficial to his ministry. There have been many interpretations concerning this *"thorn in the flesh"* that Paul is referring to in this letter. Some have said that this thorn was attributed to an issue with Paul's eyesight following his Damascus encounter. Some have attributed it to an inner emotional turmoil, and there are many other perspectives. All of the perspectives seems possible considering the evident circumstances in the life of Paul. However, I believe that what Paul had to deal with should not take the dominant focus off of the thorn. In Job's case, Satan had to acquire permission from God to afflict him. If we apply this logic to Paul it then presents the question, did God authorized this thorn? Paul refers to the thorn as *"the messenger of Satan"* that was sent to buffet him. So then it is quite apparent that God does employ opposition at times- to keep us humble. In Numbers 13, God promised Moses and the children Israel the land of Canaan. Although God promised them

Canaan, it was still their responsibility to go and possess or take the land.

However, the Amalekites, Jebusites, Amorites, and the Canaanites were still residents and occupants of the land. In other words, God permitted Israel's enemies to stay in the land that he promised them, because unbeknownst to Israel, their enemies were actually needed. The children of Israel had no real experience in keeping up their own land, planting crops, harvesting and farming. So God used their enemies (while in the land) to do all the work for them. But, here is something else interesting about this story: the land of Canaan at this time in history was also inhabited by wild animals. Particularly the lions that quite naturally the Canaanites and the other "-ites" knew how to handle and the children of Israel of course had no idea about. Now, if God would have cleared out all the children of Israel's enemies at once, and allow them just to walk into the

" Send thou men, that they may search the land of Canaan, which I give unto the children of Israel: of every tribe of their fathers shall ye send a man, every one a ruler among them."

Numbers 13:2

promised land, the lions of the land most likely would have quickly devoured them. They would not have been able to enjoy the milk and honey of the land. Now, allow me to paint the picture differently by making it personal... Think of the lions as <u>PRIDE</u>! So, evidently by this, we can see that God will sometimes use our enemies, adversities and obstacles to our advantage. This will not always present us with an easy fix. Instead it may cause us to have to participate in the process of our purpose for more than just achieving the goal, but achieving the goal while remaining humble.

Let's return back to the story for a moment...Paul prays three times to the Lord that this thorn be taken away. The Lord's reply to him is *"My grace is sufficient for thee: my strength is made perfect in weakness."* Not the ideal answer I'm sure to his request!

***

As I have experienced life more, this scripture has taken quite an impactful meaning to me. God, in his reply to Paul's request, shows his awesome long suffering toward him. How so you may say. Here is a hard truth to accept. My father told me this. *"God doesn't deliver us from everything, but rather gives us the grace we need to outgrow and/or graduate from some things."*

We must understand that there are things that are attached to us sometimes that are not altogether bad, but at the same time, not altogether good for where God is taking us in our lives. And the greatest heartbreak for us at times is having to detach ourselves from that that we've been so psychologically and emotionally attached to. Over time, that thing or person has occupied a place or space in or with us that has now become very apparent and influential in our life. Consequently, your NEXT can be crucially jeopardized by your NOW! Ultimately yet unfortunately, it was never meant for us to live our lives permanently on grace. We are to live knowing that if by chance grace is ever needed, grace is forever available. For example, if you have ever had a bill due, but you were currently between pay periods. If requested, usually a company can issue you an extension or grace period. This means that the

"God doesn't deliver us from everything, but rather gives us the grace we need to outgrow and/or graduate from some things."

company says, "*We understand that things happen sometime beyond our control, and occasionally you may need some more time to pay your bill. So we will allow you a few extra days to better your situation and then satisfy the balance of your balance with us.*" Some companies will allow no more than two or three extensions or "grace periods" in a year. They have the capability at times to be understanding. However, they will not allow their grace to be taken advantage of or mishandled-habitually.

The Bible comforts in saying that His mercies are renewed every morning. Many of us are have (more than a few times) mishandled and even taken advantage of the grace of God. When we do this we make grace our lives' constant crutch rather than an occasional aide to help us through. Therefore, we are guilty of trying to live permanently on a temporary arrangement.

After the response from God to Paul, if it were us, I believe we would have probably become very bitter. Simply because we didn't get the answer that we were looking for. Secondly, our childish resolve is that God is always supposed to say yes to our request, granting us whatever it is we've asked him to do. And, because

His response was not what was expected, we then cut back on praying to God or even acknowledging God, scale

back on our church attendance, or when we do attend, we are absent while present as if to show God that we are in our feelings. That is known as a childish adult tantrum! We are all very guilty at times of praying to God in hopes that His will lines up with our will

"For your thoughts are not my thoughts, neither are your ways my ways, saith the LORD." Isaiah 55:8 KJV

instead of the other way around. It should be our will lining up with His will. All while knowing most of the time that our will is not even anywhere in the ball park.

This scripture in 2 Corinthians 12 has always amazed me. It shows Paul being pushed into his purpose when he finally understood the purpose of his pain. Paul then embraces his thorn which was seemingly adverse in his understanding to the fulfillment of his purpose. He used it to his advantage and for God's glory. Ultimately he discovers that there is indeed strength in being weak. He equates that when he is weak then he is strong. In other words, when he found himself weak in his ability to do, the power of God through His Spirit stands up in Paul and makes him strong for the purpose of God's purpose in his life!

And we know that all things work together for good to them that love God, to them who are called according to HIS purpose. Romans 8:28 KJV

***

On Saturday morning, May 28, 2016, We awoke to the sound of Quad gagging. Immediately we rushed into his room thinking he must've gotten too full from his overnight feed. When I reached out to pick him up, he was burning up so much that he literally burnt my hand. I told Neshia to bring me the thermometer to check his temperature, because we understood that a fever that high was a risk of brain damage or even worst. His thermometer read 106.7. The night before was the commencement exercises for our school, and just before leaving home, we noticed that he appeared to be a little flushed and warm. We took his temperature and it read 102.3. After giving him Tylenol, the fever dropped back down to normal, assuming he had maybe started contracting a cold or possibly just a sinus infection.

That morning, we immediately got dressed and rushed him to the emergency room. After getting there and going through triage and to a room, the ER physician came in to check his vitals, etc. You know the drill; temperature, heart rate, blood pressure, eyes, and ears. When the ER physician looked in the back of Quad's mouth, she jumped back and with a look of disgust she said, "His tonsils are very inflamed, white, and full of puss. We're going to test him for strep throat, the flu and tonsillitis. How long has he been feeling like this," she asked. She concluded that he must have had this for several weeks. For those of you that don't know, Quad cannot really talk. This small detail kind of leaves us in the dark a lot of times. Simply because he can't just tell us what is going on with him. Most times we have to read what little amount of gesture he gives and try our best to figure it out. He's pretty much a happy-go-lucky kid, but when he's not..., you would know that there is indeed a problem. So when she said that, my heart drop to the floor. All I could think about at that moment was him being in such terrible pain maybe weeks without the ability to voice how or what he's feeling.

The results came back from the strep, the flu and tonsillitis tests, all of which were negative. The doctor then tested him for Mononucleosis or "Mono". Mono is an infectious virus also called the "kissing disease" because it is commonly spread through the saliva. But

" All I could think about at that moment was him being in such terrible pain maybe weeks..."

guess what? That test results were negative as well. They decided to put him on antibiotics and keep him overnight for observation and release him on Sunday. After admitting him and getting him in his room, it seem as though this was one of his regular visits, but that was so far from what we imagined. By that evening, he had developed this very nasty cough and his breathing began to decrease. They put him on oxygen, but his stats continued to decrease. The next morning, the doctor ordered X-rays and discovered he had something called adenovirus. Adenovirus can cause a wide range of illnesses such as a common cold, sore throat, bronchitis, pneumonia, diarrhea, pink eye (conjunctivitis), severe fever, bladder infection, gastroenteritis (inflammation of the stomach and intestines) and neurological disease (conditions that affect the brain and spinal cord). Bingo!

He was then quickly transferred to the Pediatric Intensive Care Unit (PICU), where they began invasive treatment. They increased his oxygen to 100%, but it was still not working. His oxygen level continued to decline. So they decided to put him on a Bi-PAP (Bi-level Positive Airway Pressure) machine which sends increased air pressure through a mask to ensure his airways don't collapse. It seemed as though everything that they tried was unsuccessful. The next day, the PICU doctor came and sat with us to tell us what was going on. He said, *"James is not doing good at all, but we're going to do everything possible to get this little guy back to you."* Whatever you're thinking right now…, we were thinking the same thing. The doctor began to explain to us, *"After looking at his X-rays, there are a number of things that we're very concerned about. His lungs are in very bad shape"*, he said. *"Both have collapsed, and there is a lot of damage and scarring to them, which is the reason for the low stats in his breathing. He also has a very severe case of pneumonia which explains the fluid in both lungs. We see that he has only one kidney. His kidney function is very low, due to the antibiotics not being strong enough to fight this virus, which has now cause his blood pressure to drastically decline. We are ordering 3 different medicines for him to try and bring his pressure back to his baseline,"*. As he spoke I noticed him looking at us with that look that said, "I really don't want to tell these people their child isn't going to make it." Again, we were devastated. Our child; same child; different situation, but the same feeling. *"We are going to have to do an intubation procedure*, the doctor says. *"This is where we will insert a breathing tube into his mouth and down to his lungs. The oscillator machine will inflate and deflate his lungs. He will have to be sedated, because this virus was very aggressive and has taken over his entire body. We don't want him to breathe on his own. We want him to rest and preserve his strength while the antibiotics and other drips work. Mr. and Mrs. Brant, we are going to do everything possible. Let's keep our fingers crossed. Hopefully with a lot of prayer and time, he may pull through."* We were then asked to wait in the waiting room while they prepped him and perform the intubation procedure. All of our family and church family were there in the waiting room for prayer and support. After about an hour, the nurse came out to let us know that the procedure was successful, and we could go back and see him if we wanted to. Neshia and I rushed back to see him. When we got back there and saw him laying in there with all these tubes, valves coming out of him, too many medicines to count, this big machine hooked to his seemingly lifeless body…, I totally lost it. I left the room in a panic; out the door, pass the waiting room, and outside. My father, mother, and Neshia

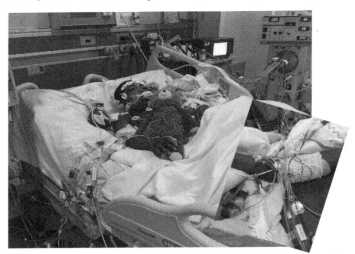

came walking out behind me. Neshia was crying and trying to console me at the same time. My father said, "Son, everything is going to be okay. We still believe God and whatever His will is in this situation…"

Every day's update of Quad's condition following the procedure was basically the same, *"Mr. and Mrs. Brant, there are no changes as of yet."* After daily X-rays of his lungs, adding medicines, doing this and doing that; trying this and trying that..., no change. Neshia and I began to come to grips with reality; maybe Quad was not going to make it out of this one. Maybe this is it this time. I talked to my father about it. And seeing how messed up we were about it, he said to me. *"Well James, if this is in fact it; if God decides to take him, Quad has had an amazing life; nine years. You and Neshia have been awesome parents, and Quad couldn't have had better parents than you two, and we're very proud of you two. Let God do what He's gonna do. All I ask of you two is that you not allow those doctors or everybody else to make my grandson a guinea pig, experimenting with this and experimenting with that."* I believe that after that conversation with my father, I had kind of given up. Neshia and I began to talk about making funeral plans, and how we wanted his service to be: who would get his body, what he would wear, who would sing, who would do the eulogy, etc.

Fast forwarding a bit. About thirteen days in and still no change, however, this particular day was different than all the rest. Everybody was still supporting us and coming to the hospital, sitting and waiting in the waiting room with us for extended hours, but this particular day my father wanted to go back and see Quad. He would normally just wait in the waiting room with everyone else, talking, but this time he decided to come back to Quad's room. Now, my father had only seen him one time since the procedure, and that time, he just stood at the door on the outside of the room. But this time, he actually walked into the room. He went to Quad's bedside and grabbed his hand. Immediately, as I saw it, I whispered to my mother, and Neshia, "*Let's step out and give them some time alone.*" So we stood outside of the room talking. I can remember my father's back was turned to us. I knew that he must've been praying, but I couldn't hear him. After a few minutes, he comes out of the room and says, "*Alright Denise, you ready to go get some lunch? We'll check with y'all a little bit later,*" and they left.

That Sunday morning in church, the service was awesome. My father told the congregation a little about Quad's situation and how it has always been his prayer since Quad was born that God would work a miracle in his life. Then he said something that still gives me chills to this day. He said, "*I told the Lord that even if it cost my life, I want Him to heal my grandson.*" I immediately rehearsed back in my mind that day that my father was in the room with Quad. A few days later, Quad's stats began to drastically change and normalize. They began taking him off all those medicines one-by-one. His eyes were open. The ventilator tube was removed. He was then transferred to a regular room and then a few days later released to go home. We were so blown away at how God turned things around so quickly, but not knowing the true cost of this miracle. Quad was released on June 17, 2016 and my father passed on Sunday, July 10, 2016. Not even a month later and just three days before Quad's tenth birthday. Trust me, you can't even imagine the pain, the agony, the confusion, the anger, and the helplessness we felt. It was as though our whole world was stripped from us at the blink of an eye.

The sudden passing of my father was very devastating to many; not only our family and our local church, but internationally. No one could've ever fathomed this travesty. It was not until later as I remember the day that my father went into Quad's room and that Sunday that I somewhat understood how this whole thing came about. I asked God, "*Out of all the many prayers I'm sure that my father had ever prayed in his fifty-eight years of life; all the prayers that had not yet been answered, why in the world* (I may have used another word there; I'm not really sure) *would you choose to answer that prayer; an exchange; his life for Quad's life?*" God honored his request! At that moment, I was so confused, frustrated, angry and felt guilty, because it almost seemed as though emotionally, I needed to choose. On one hand, my son is alive and I should be grateful. The flip side was my father thought enough of his first grandson his namesake, to give his life in exchange. I was already prepared for my son to die, but not my father. How would you feel? Which one would you choose?

Everyone says hindsight is 20/20. Looking back on the life of my father and how he raised my brothers and I, and the lessons and the wisdom he constantly imparted into us, not only by word, but deed and actions, he was preparing us all that time for his departure. I have six brothers and we all work full-time in ministry since 2006 alongside our parents. All six of us have a particular trait of my father. Not one of us embody him totally, but together, we makeup who my father is. Crazy huh? Therefore, it has

" All six of us have a particular trait of my father. Not one of us embody him totally, but together, we makeup who my father is."

really helped my mother tremendously, because she sees the embodiment of her husband in all of their sons every day. Of course, we could never equal those thirty-eight years, his presence, and his touch… Most of us who have been in church for a while and have attended a few funerals are familiar with John 14.

It is commonly used as the New Testament reading in almost every funeral setting. It is totally the opposite of the funeral setting scripture when it's put in its proper context. First of all, when reading the

Bible, you must understand that it is separated by chapters. The chapter separation was primarily done by the translator in order for the reader's mind to process truth, but in segments. For example: if I'm conversing with someone, I would not break my conversation up into chapters. So part of the challenge we have with Bible reading is that sometimes because of chapters, we cease to put things together that are meant to continue; thought as well as idea.

So John 14 begins with *"Let not your heart be troubled"*, which means that you have been dropped right in the middle of a conversation. The conversation did not begin with *"Let not your heart be troubled"*. It is actually the response to John 13:31-38.

[31] When he had gone out, Jesus said, "Now is the Son of Man glorified, and God is glorified in him. [32] If God is glorified in him, God will also glorify him in himself, and glorify him at once. [33] Little children, yet a little while I am with you. You will seek me, and just as I said to the Jews, so now I also say to you, 'Where I am going you cannot come.' [34] A new commandment I give to you, that you love one another: just as I have loved you, you also are to love one another. [35] By this all

people will know that you are my disciples, if you have love for one another." [36] Simon Peter said to him, "Lord, where are you going?" Jesus answered him, "Where I am going you cannot follow me now, but you will follow afterward." [37] Peter said to him, "Lord, why can I not follow you now? I will lay down my life for you." [38] Jesus answered, "Will you lay down your life for me? Truly, truly, I say to you, the rooster will not crow till you have denied me three times.

John 13:31-38 ESV

This was actually a conversation between Jesus and Peter. Peter expressed his loyalty to Jesus and how he would follow Him wherever He went, and even to the extent of how he would even die for Jesus. It sounded good in the heat of the moment. However, Jesus then introduces Peter to his future and tells him that his loyalty is about to be tested and he's going to fail; he denying Jesus three times before the rooster crowed. Then, in the first verse of the next chapter, Jesus comforts Peter to not allow what will happen next to cause him to feel unqualified, disqualified, or even inadequate. But then Jesus begins talking about mansions in his Father's house and going away to prepare a place. And it is almost as if to ask, "What does that have to do with anything?" Well, let me see if I can't explain this a little more clearer.

The Father's house was a reference to the temple, and the temple was the dwelling place of God and his presence. But when Jesus died, the temple's door were flung open and the curtain was torn from top to bottom and the way to God's presence had now been opened for all to enter. Now, we are the temple of God and His presence dwells in us.

When we see the word "mansions" in John 14, it is not suggestive of our perceptive image or concept of what a mansion is; you know, the six bedrooms, eight bathrooms, six-car garage, the home theater..., etc. No. The word mansion in the Greek interpretation is referred to as many rooms or spaces. Sorry, there are no mansions in the sky.

And if I go and prepare a place for you, I will come again, and receive you unto myself; that where I am, there ye may be also.

John 14:3 KJV

He tells the disciples, *"I go to prepare a place for you. And if I go and prepare a place for you, I will come again..."*

So wait! If Jesus says *"I go to prepare a place for you,"* but Genesis tells us that God finished all his work by day six of creation and rested on the seventh day, then what was Jesus referring to when he said *I go to prepare a place for you*? It would look as if to imply that he's leaving here to finish a heavenly construction project that somehow wasn't finished on day six.

Now, picture this: if I go away, but you stay here, and I come back, then where are we? It's not a trick question. If I went <u>there</u> to prepare a place for you, and came back <u>here</u>, but you never left <u>here</u>, then that means that both of us are <u>here</u>, right? Could it be that the place that He was preparing for Peter was not there, but here? Could it be that this place He was referring to was not at all a celestial estate or *"heavenly"* geographical location?

Jesus tells his disciples that by dying and being raised from the dead, He will go and prepare a place or room, or space for them. Once atonement for our sins have been made, then the way will be opened and there will be room for everyone; every person, culture, color, and tongue.

***

On July 8th, the Friday night before my father passed, I had the opportunity to sit with my father all night at his bedside. He was in a lot of pain that night so I didn't want to leave until he was able to go to sleep. He never went to sleep and I never left. We talked all night. Well, he did most of the talking, and I listened, not knowing that that night would be the last time I would ever have a conversation with my father. He shared some things with me, so many nuggets of wisdom that maybe he understood that I could only use in his absence. It almost seemed as if he knew that he was not going to make it. Because of the morphine, his speech was slurred, and he would often say some weird things. So being the funny man I am, and coming from a family of funny people, I decided to record my father and his shenanigans so I could play it for my brothers when we all came together at Sunday dinner, not knowing that it would be the very last time that my father would ever speak. Here was a man, perfectly healthy, in the hospital with just a pain in his foot and now two days later…

As I reminisce on all that my father was to us and everything that he taught us. I believe that his life in my opinion was so synonymous to this scripture. Now, when I look at who we are and where we are and what we have become in the absence of my father, we never could've been who and where we are had he not been gone. We were present with my father, but in his shadow. I've never known a tree or flower that can grow and blossom to its fullest potential in the shadows. It is impossible. But when there is nothing between the sunlight and tree and they finally meet face to face, that tree can grow big and strong and blossom to become what it was originally designated to become.

"But when there is nothing between the sunlight and tree and they finally meet face to face, that tree can grow big and strong and blossom to become what it was originally designated to become."

My father prepared this place *(space)* for us. There were things that he imparted to each of us that wouldn't have been activated in his presence. This is because there was no need for activation with him being present. One of our longtime friends, Apostle Lillie Tuggerson told me how proud she was of me after I was elevated to the position of executive pastor at our church. My reply was *"Well Apostle, I really want to do well and lead God's people. I'm praying for wisdom…"* She said to me, *"You're wasting your time son. You don't ever have to pray for wisdom when your father is still present. You pray for wisdom when he's no longer here."*

So these experiences in my life have really taught me that God doesn't always use pretty things to manifest his purpose. Purpose for our lives come gift wrapped sometimes with pain and pressure. Never think that you'll ever get through life with manicured hands and pedicured feet when even Jesus himself had holes in his! It is then up to us no matter how difficult it is or will become, to embrace our pain. The purpose will always and forever outweigh it all.

"…weeping may endure for a night, but joy cometh in the morning." Psalms 30:5 KJV

And we know that all things work together

for good to them that love God, to them

who are the called according to his purpose.

Romans 8:28 KJV

THE BOOK OF JAMES
X-RAY FINDING PURPOSE IN PAIN

ABOUT THE AUTHOR

James Brant III, a husband, a father, a preacher, a pastor, a talented musician and singer, and the firstborn son of six sons and two adopted sons, is a humble native of Jacksonville, Florida.

Being raised in a household where his parents having pastored more than thirty years, it is safe to say he has been in church all his life. He currently serves as the executive pastor of the Zarephath Tabernacle Church in Jacksonville, Florida, where his father and mother founded and have pastored there for more than twenty years.

In his debut book, "The Book of James", he shares transparently some of his life's challenges, struggles, tragedies, and triumphs, and how he examined his own life to find purpose in those things that had proven very painful rather than searching for the cause and a cure for the pain.

62378049R00071

Made in the USA
Columbia, SC
02 July 2019